THE BIG BOOK OF
ACTIVITIES

Peg Connery-Boyd

Illustrations by Scott Waddell

Published by Sourcebooks Jabberwocky, an imprint of Sourcebooks, Inc.
P.O. Box 4410, Naperville, Illinois 60567-4410
(630) 961-3900
Fax: (630) 961-2168
www.sourcebooks.com

Originally published in 2012 as *Red Sox Activity Book* in the United States of America by
Hawk's Nest Publishing, LLC.

Source of production: Versa Press, East Peoria, Illinois, USA
Date of production: February 2016
Run number: 5005810

Printed and bound in the United States of America.
VP 10 9 8 7 6 5 4 3 2 1

WALLY THE GREEN MONSTER™

TM

RETIRED HEROES

Unscramble the names of the *Red Sox* heroes
on the jerseys below.

NOCRIN
4

CRONIN
_____

SEPKY
6

_____

ZEMYASTRSKI
8

_____

ALMIWILS
9

_____

SIFK
27

_____

CERI
14

_____

Solution is on page 49.

FOLLOW THE BALL
Which pitcher threw the strike?

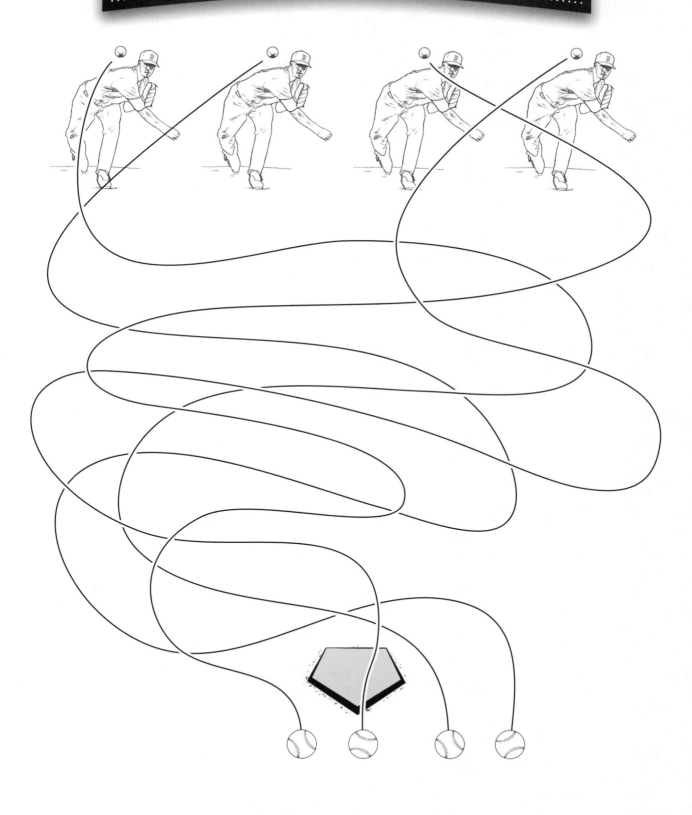

Solution is on page 49.

CONNECT THE DOTS

BOSTON RED SOX™

HINT!
A true *Red Sox* fan never leaves home without it!

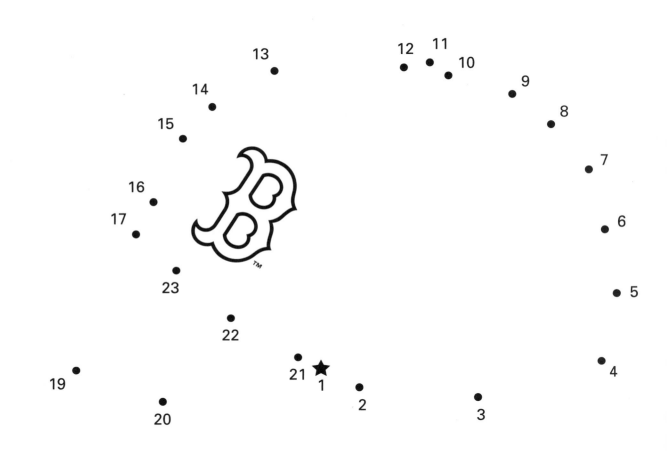

13

12 11
    10

14

9

15

8

7

16

6

17

5

18

23

4

22

21 1

19

2

3

20

FIND THE DIFFERENCES

Can you find all **three** differences between the two images below?

Solution is on page 50.

START HERE

Solution is on page 50.

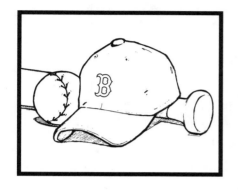 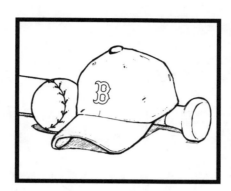 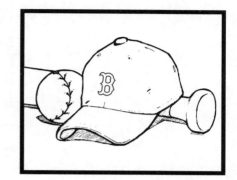

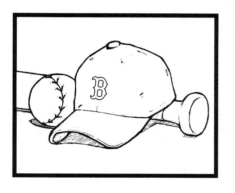 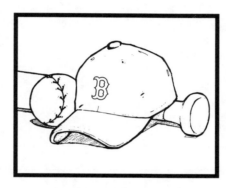 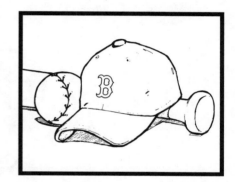

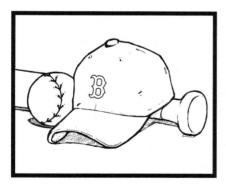  

LET'S DRAW!

Use the grid to draw the *Red Sox* logo.

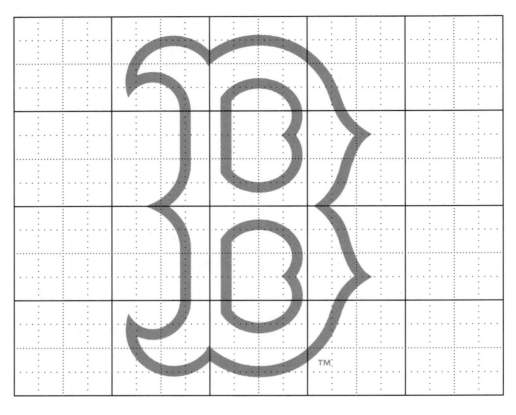

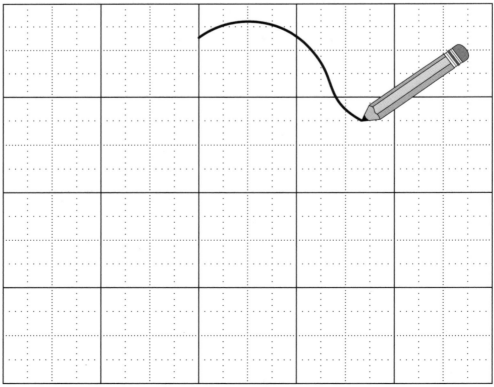

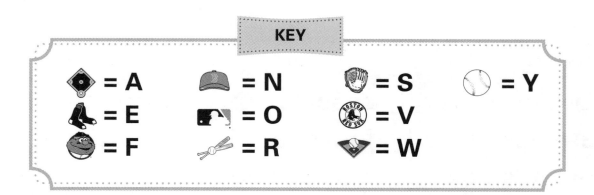

KEY

= A	= N	= S	= Y
= E	= O	= V	
= F	= R	= W	

Solution is on page 51.

LABEL THE PARTS OF A BASEBALL FIELD

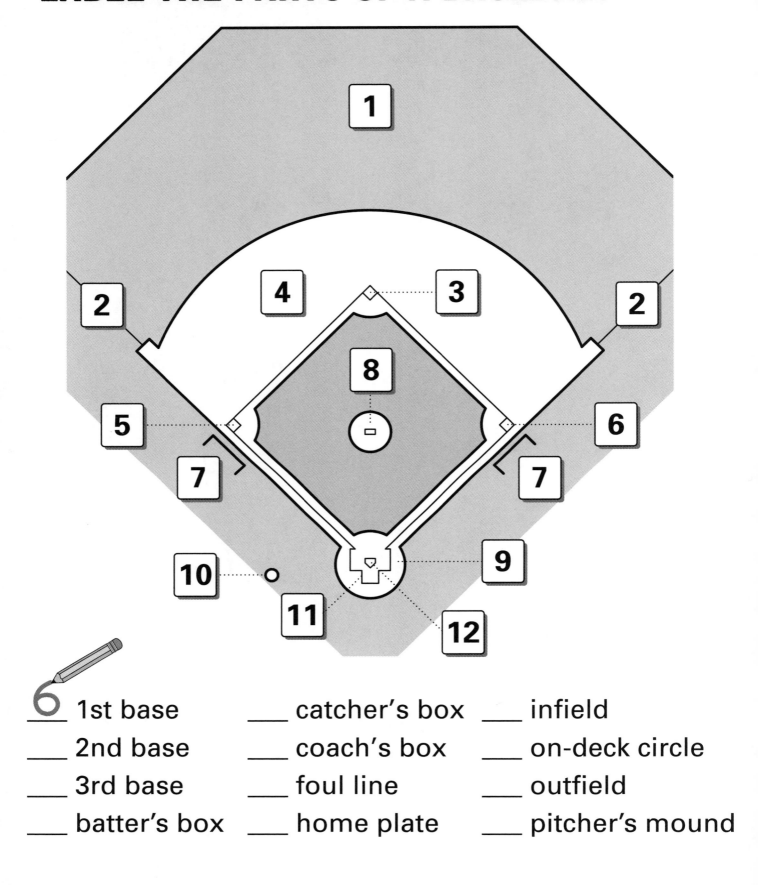

___ 1st base   ___ catcher's box   ___ infield

___ 2nd base   ___ coach's box   ___ on-deck circle

___ 3rd base   ___ foul line   ___ outfield

___ batter's box   ___ home plate   ___ pitcher's mound

SCRAMBLE

Unscramble the letters of these *Fenway Park*™ snacks.

DOAS

_ _ _ _

OTH GDO

_ _ _ _ _ _

ROCPOPN

_ _ _ _ _ _ _

CIE MCEAR

_ _ _ _ _ _ _ _

ZEPRTEL

_ _ _ _ _ _ _

NUPTEAS

_ _ _ _ _ _ _

Solution is on page 52.

CONNECT THE DOTS

BOSTON RED SOX™

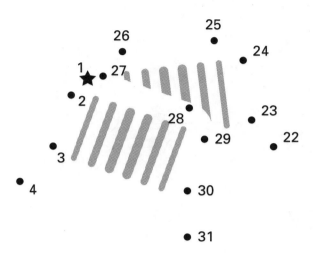

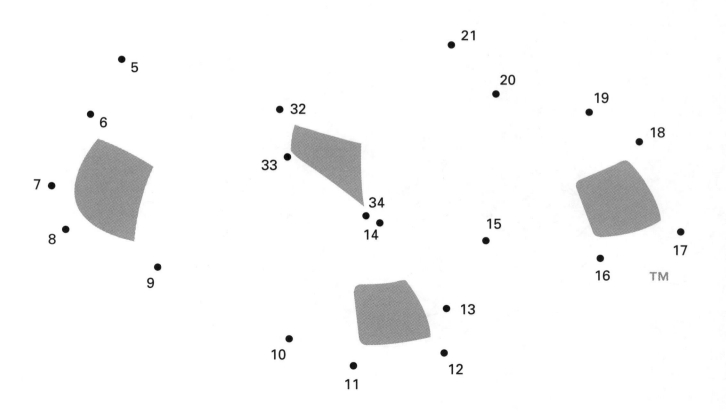

TM

WORD SEARCH

```
D M O N S T E R S L A
Y A S T R Z E M S K I
A Q E U W C R A R N D
W B B R N I W A L L Y
K B M O W Z P C N D W
E F R N S Y C O U I I
Y I P E A T I E F L V
W S O W D T O A R A D
A K N G A S X N H W P
Y E B N A U O K M W T
F Z M I M O B X X D G
```

BOSTON	MONSTER	WALLY
FENWAY PARK	NATION	YASTRZEMSKI
FISK	RED SOX	YAWKEY WAY

Solution is on page 53.

BATTER UP!

CROSSWORD PUZZLE
Use your knowledge of baseball
to solve the puzzle.

Across

1. The pitcher stands on the pitcher's _____ when he throws the baseball.

5. After the batter hits the ball, he runs toward _____ base.

6. The player who throws the ball toward home plate for the batter to hit is called the _____.

9. To score a run, the player must touch _____ plate.

Down

2. The _____ calls the balls and strikes.

3. Each baseball player wears a baseball _____ on his head.

4. Three strikes and you're _____!

7. The player who crouches behind home plate is called the _____.

8. A baseball player wears a _____ on his hand to catch the ball.

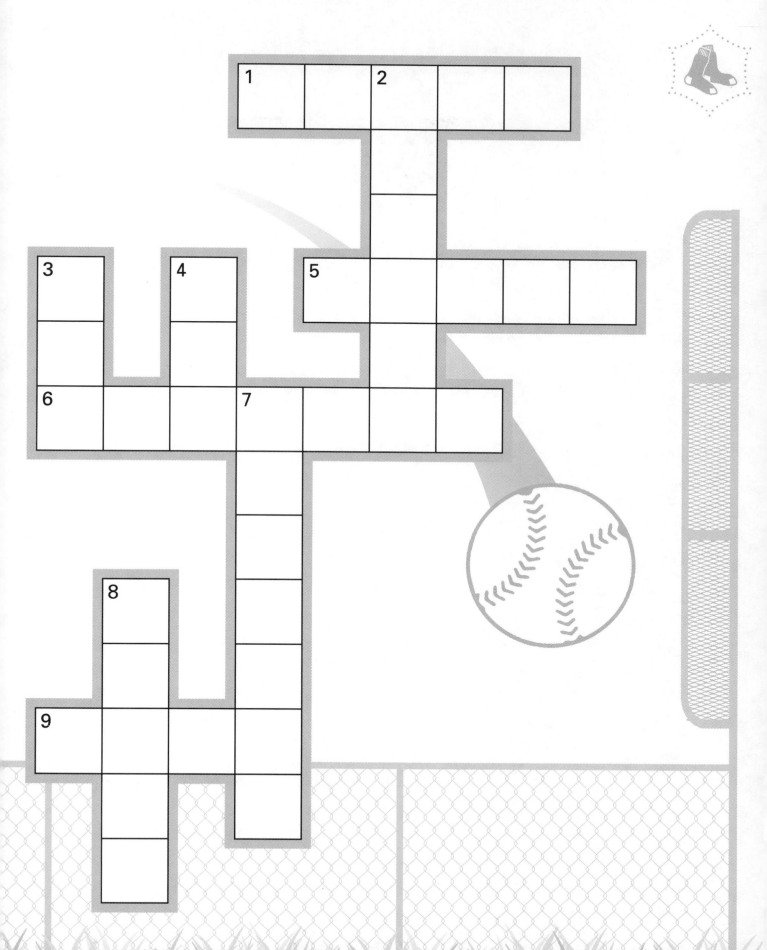

CONNECT THE DOTS

BOSTON RED SOX

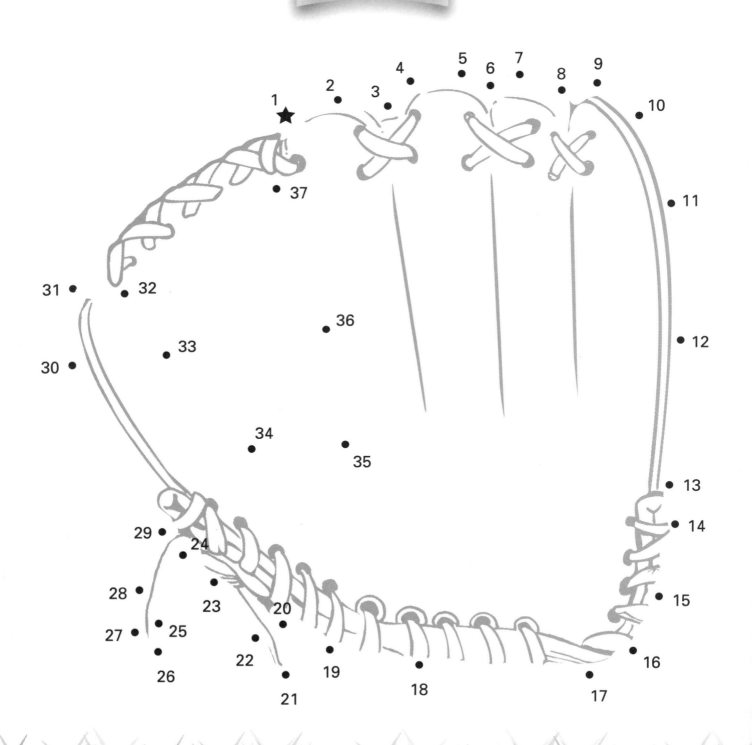

I HAD A GREAT DAY AT **FENWAY PARK**

by _____
(your name)

It was a _____ day in _____.
(weather word)   (month)

The *Red Sox* were playing the _____ at
(team name)

Fenway Park. We took a _____ to get to
(car / train / bus)

Boston. I snacked on some _____ and
(food)

_____ while we watched the game. I was
(food)

so excited to see _____ play
(player name)

today. He's my favorite player! The *Red Sox*

_____ the game. The score was ____ to ____.
(won / lost)   (score)   (score)

Baseball is my favorite sport, but I also like to

watch _____. I can't wait to come back
(sport)

to *Fenway Park*!

A HOME RUN FOR THE RED SOX!

SCRAMBLE

Unscramble the letters of these baseball words.

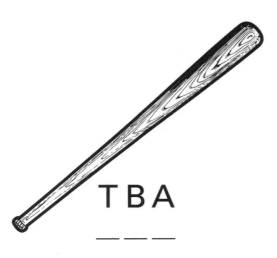

TBA

_ _ _

APC

_ _ _

PMRIEU

_ _ _ _ _ _

SYERJE

_ _ _ _ _ _

VOEGL

_ _ _ _ _

EBAS

_ _ _ _

FOLLOW THE BALL

The outfielder is about to make a catch!
Which batter will be out?

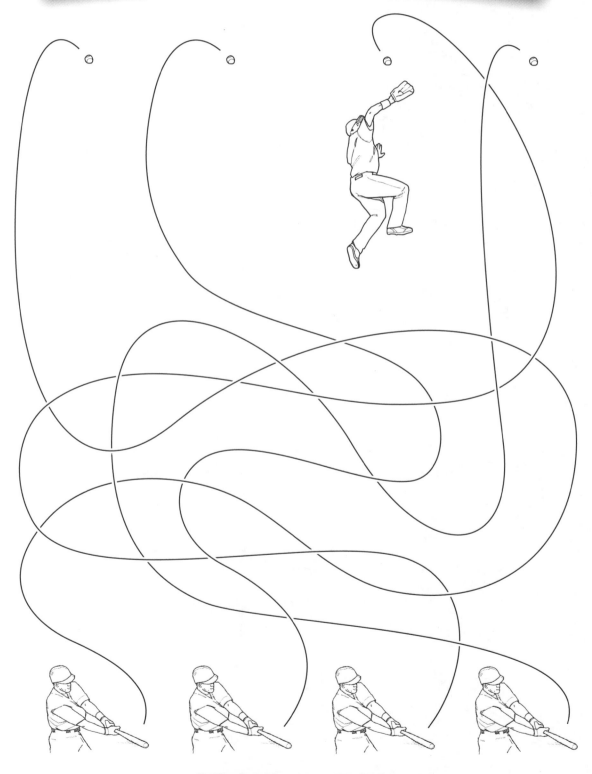

Solution is on page 54.

KEY

= C	= H	= R	= V
= E	= I	= S	
= G	= N	= T	

Solution is on page 55.

WORD SEARCH

```
T T P L A Y O F F S D
E W U T H I D E N N N
O S E P F G C O S A B
B E O N W Y I R C S A
F R L U A P A I J G L
T I M D M T R U Q B L
H E V A S E I Y W F P
D S H L M F B O L X A
Y C L A A R Z U N W R
C A F L E Y X Q Q A K
V S S S D E R O Z O U L
```

ALL STARS	CHAMPIONS	PLAYOFFS
AMERICAN	DERBY	SERIES
BALLPARK	NATIONAL	TROPHY

Solution is on page 55.

HIDDEN PICTURE

Use the key to color the shapes below and reveal the hidden picture.

KEY

A = Brown   **B = Blue**   **C = Purple**   **D = Green**   **E = Yellow**   **F = Black**

HINT!
Color inside the lines!

SECRET MESSAGE
Use the key to decode the message.

THREE

STRIKES,

AND YOU'RE

OUT!

KEY

= A	= H	= N	= S	= Y
= D	= I	= O	= T	
= E	= K	= R	= U	

Solution is on page 56.

29

RED SOX™

B™

BOSTON™

WHAT'S IN A NAME?

How many words can you make using letters found in the three words below?

B O S T O N   R E D   S O X

Example: ROBOT

ROSE

1 _____

2 _____

3 _____

4 _____

5 _____

6 _____

7 _____

8 _____

9 _____

10 _____

11 _____

12 _____

13 _____

14 _____

15 _____

16 _____

17 _____

18 _____

19 _____

20 _____

Solution is on page 56.

MY BASEBALL CARD

SIDE 1:
Draw yourself!

_____
(your name)

#
_____
(number)

RED SOX™

SIDE 2:
Complete your stats!

RED SOX™

Age: _____

Position: _____

Height: _____

Weight: _____

Circle one!

I bat (righty / lefty)
I throw (righty / lefty)

_____ has shown excellent
(your name)
sportsmanship this year!

32

WHAT'S THE SCORE?

Add the runs to find out which team won the game.

Example:	1	2	3	4	5	6	7	8	9	R
ORIOLES	0	1	0	0	2	0	0	0	0	3
RED SOX	0	0	1	0	0	1	0	0	2	4

Game 1:	1	2	3	4	5	6	7	8	9	R
ORIOLES	0	0	0	0	1	0	2	0	0	
RED SOX	0	2	0	0	1	0	1	1	0	

Game 2:	1	2	3	4	5	6	7	8	9	R
YANKEES	0	0	1	0	0	0	0	0	1	
RED SOX	0	3	0	0	2	0	0	2	0	

Game 3:	1	2	3	4	5	6	7	8	9	R
RAYS	0	3	1	2	0	1	0	1	0	
RED SOX	0	1	0	1	2	0	1	0	1	

Game 4:	1	2	3	4	5	6	7	8	9	R
BLUE JAYS	1	1	1	0	1	0	3	0	0	
RED SOX	0	4	1	0	1	1	0	0	2	

Solution is on page 57.

START HERE

LET'S DRAW!
Use the grid to draw the *MLB*™ logo.

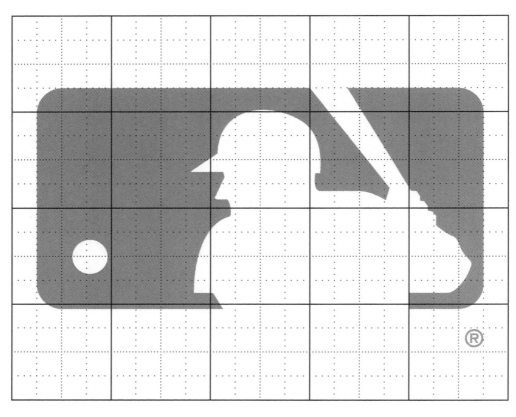

®

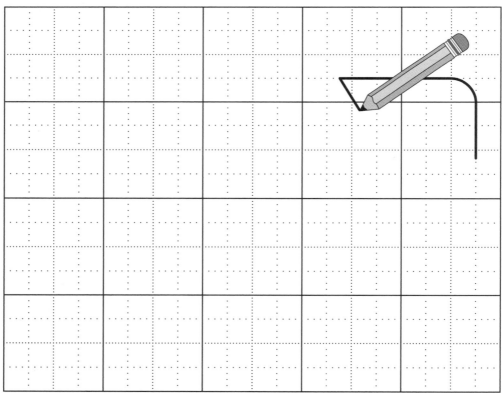

WORD SEARCH

```
H Y W I L L I A M S D
I A C M F Z M I Y G A
R S B C T C F F K X L
J T R O Y E R P X J W
I R E A G E F O Y I J
O Z I C E G F K N X Q
B E C C Y Y S I J I V
Q M Q I E E U U S O N
Y S S Z P X N Q Q K K
P K E X O V Y U I A N
E I F Z H K D O E R R
```

BOGGS	FISK	RICE
CRONIN	FOXX	WILLIAMS
DOERR	PESKY	YASTRZEMSKI

Solution is on page 58.

ONE LUCKY
RED SOX FAN

SECRET MESSAGE
Use the key to decode the message.

T A K E   M E

O U T   T O   T H E

B A L L G A M E

KEY			
= A	= G	= L	= T
= B	= H	= M	= U
= E	= K	= O	

Solution is on page 58.

FIND THE DIFFERENCES

Can you find all **four** differences between the two images below?

Solution is on page 59.

SCRAMBLE
Unscramble the letters of these baseball positions.

ITCHREP

PITCHER

CAHTERC

_ _ _ _ _ _ _

RIFTS

_ _ _ _ _

SABMANE

_ _ _ _ _ _ _

ERTTAB

_ _ _ _ _ _

TUOLIEFDRE

_ _ _ _ _ _ _ _ _ _

Solution is on page 59.

WHAT'S IN A NAME?

How many words can you make using letters found in the three words below?

MAJOR LEAGUE BASEBALL

Example: AREA   BEAR

1 _____   11 _____

2 _____   12 _____

3 _____   13 _____

4 _____   14 _____

5 _____   15 _____

6 _____   16 _____

7 _____   17 _____

8 _____   18 _____

9 _____   19 _____

10 _____   20 _____

          Solution is on page 60.

IS THE BATTER SAFE?

Follow the maze to find out!

OUT!

SAFE!

START HERE

CROSSWORD PUZZLE

Use your knowledge of the
Red Sox to solve the puzzle.

Across

4. The beloved *Red Sox* mascot is named
   _____ *the Green Monster*.

6. *Fenway Park* is located in the part of
   Boston known as the _____ Square.

7. The famous wall in left field at *Fenway
   Park* is nicknamed "The Green _____."

Down

1. The right field foul pole at *Fenway Park* is
   named after *Red Sox* Hall of Famer Johnny
   _____.

2. Cy Young, Bill Lee, and Luis Tiant were all
   famous *Red Sox* _____.

3. The address of *Fenway Park* is 4 _____
   Way, Boston, MA 02215.

5. The _____ are the biggest rivals of the
   Red Sox.

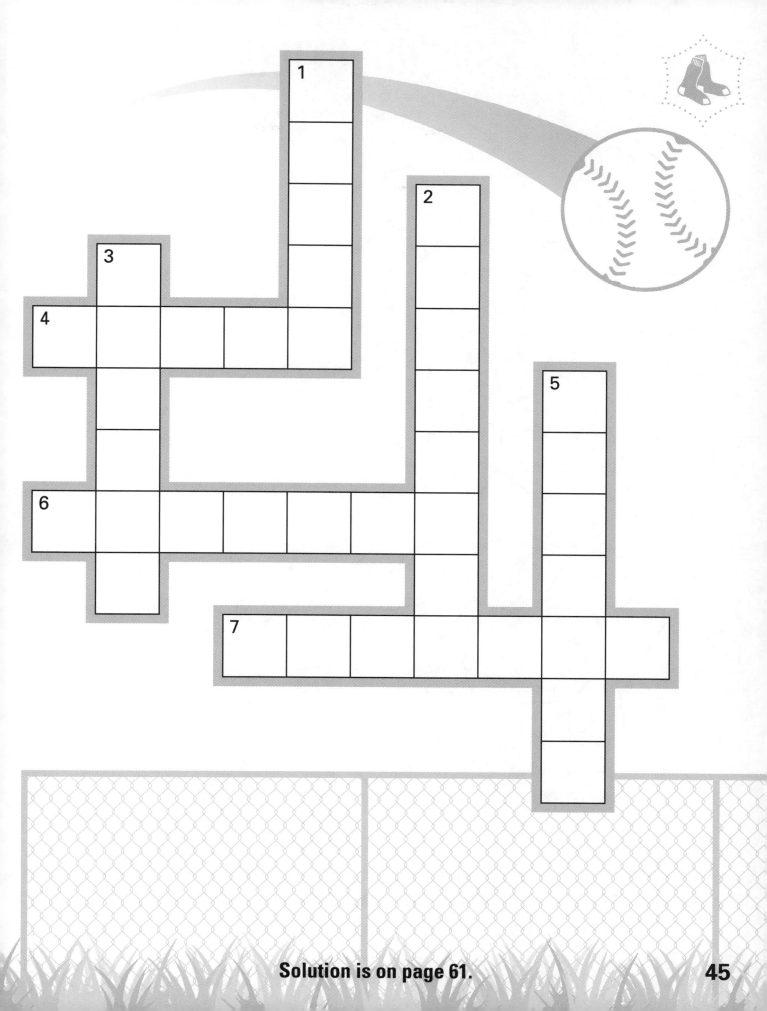

HIDDEN PICTURE

Use the key to color the shapes below and reveal the hidden picture.

KEY

A = Dark Blue   **B = Light Blue**   **C = Light Gray**   **D = Dark Gray (or black)**   **E = Tan**

HINT!
Color inside the lines!

WORD SEARCH

C T J I Q U E K R R W
P A I U D L Z K T L V
E M T G P U H C U P B
N Z S C M B G O A T A
U P Y T H L F O K P S
C C D U R E Y B U I E
F V W U R I R S I T B
O W K I O V K E R C A
Q X P G L O V E Q H L
E M Z D R G Z X T E L
U Z S O G S M T N R Q

BASEBALL   DUGOUT   PITCHER
CAP   FOUL   STRIKE
CATCHER   GLOVE   UMPIRE

Solution is on page 61.

FIND THE DIFFERENCES

Can you find all **four** differences between the two images below?

Solution is on page 62.

SOLUTIONS

Page 2

Page 3

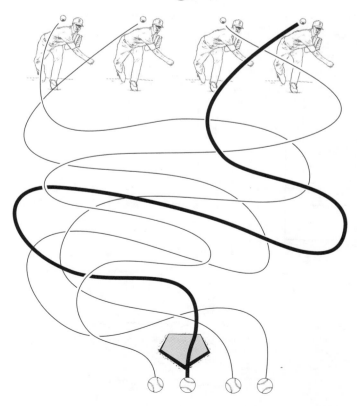

Page 5

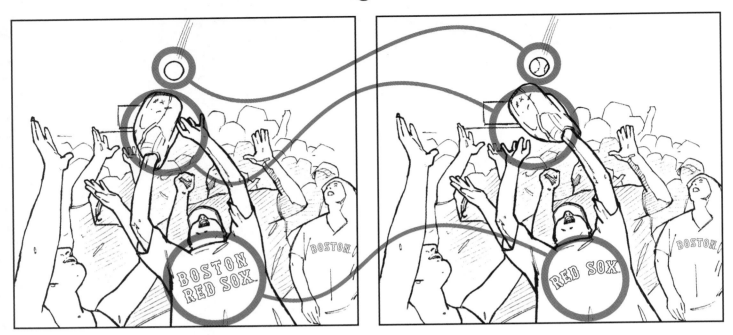

Page 6

Page 7

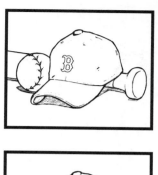 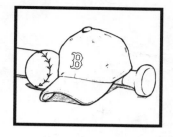 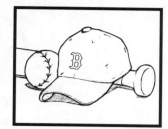

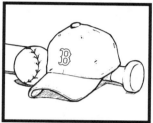 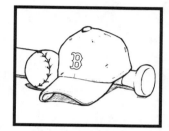 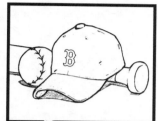

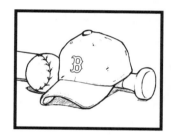 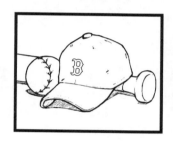 

Page 9

F E N W A Y

F A N S   A R E

F O R E V E R

Page 10

6 1st base

3 2nd base

5 3rd base

9 batter's box

11 catcher's box

7 coach's box

2 foul line

12 home plate

4 infield

10 on-deck circle

1 outfield

8 pitcher's mound

Page 12

SODA

HOT DOG

POPCORN

PRETZEL

ICE CREAM

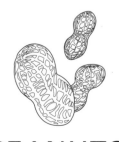

PEANUTS

Page 16

Page 19

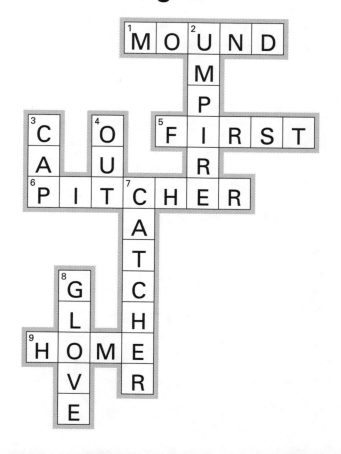

Page 24

BAT

CAP

UMPIRE

JERSEY

GLOVE

BASE

Page 25

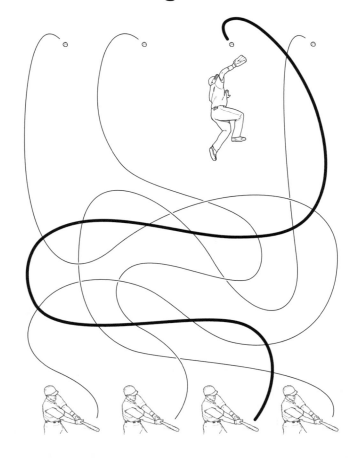

SEVENTH

INNING

STRETCH

Page 27

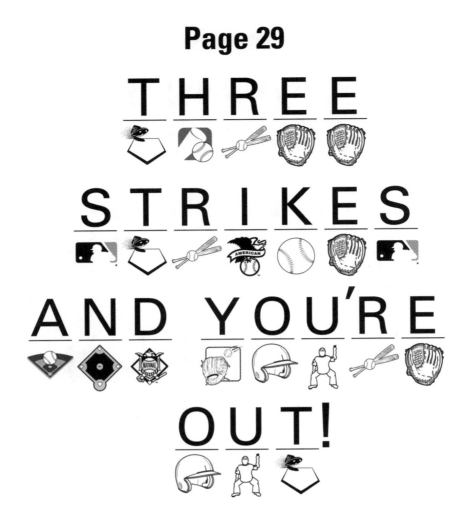

T H R E E
S T R I K E S
A N D   Y O U ' R E
O U T !

Page 31

Below are just a few examples of words that could be made with these letters.

B O S T O N   R E D   S O X

bed	bore	does	next	robe	set	stood
bend	bored	done	node	robot	snob	store
bent	born	donor	nose	rod	snore	strobe
best	boss	door	note	rodent	son	tend
bond	box	dose	odor	rodeo	soon	tone
bone	bred	end	one	root	sore	toon
boost	debt	nerd	onto	rose	sort	tore
boosted	den	nest	rent	send	stern	toss
boot	dent	net	rest	sent	stone	trend

Page 34

Game 1:	1	2	3	4	5	6	7	8	9	R
ORIOLES	0	0	0	0	1	0	2	0	0	3
RED SOX	0	2	0	0	1	0	1	1	0	5

Game 2:	1	2	3	4	5	6	7	8	9	R
YANKEES	0	0	1	0	0	0	0	0	1	2
RED SOX	0	3	0	0	2	0	0	2	0	7

Game 3:	1	2	3	4	5	6	7	8	9	R
RAYS	0	3	1	2	0	1	0	1	0	8
RED SOX	0	1	0	1	2	0	1	0	1	6

Game 4:	1	2	3	4	5	6	7	8	9	R
BLUE JAYS	1	1	1	0	1	0	3	0	0	7
RED SOX	0	4	1	0	1	1	0	0	2	9

Page 35

Page 37

Page 39

TAKE ME

OUT TO THE

BALLGAME

Page 40

Page 41

<u>P I T C H E R</u>

<u>F I R S T
B A S E M A N</u>

<u>C A T C H E R</u>

<u>B A T T E R</u>

<u>O U T F I E L D E R</u>

Page 42

Below are just a few examples of words that could be made with these letters.

M A J O R   L E A G U E   B A S E B A L L

ajar	beam	bull	gore	meal	reel	seem
alas	bear	ease	lamb	mole	roll	sell
also	bell	else	lame	mule	rule	slab
area	blob	game	lobe	muse	saga	slam
aura	blue	gear	lube	ogre	sage	soar
ball	blur	germ	lure	oral	sale	some
barb	boar	glee	male	rage	seal	sour
bare	bomb	glue	mall	real	seam	urge
base	bulb	goal	mars	ream	sear	user

Page 43

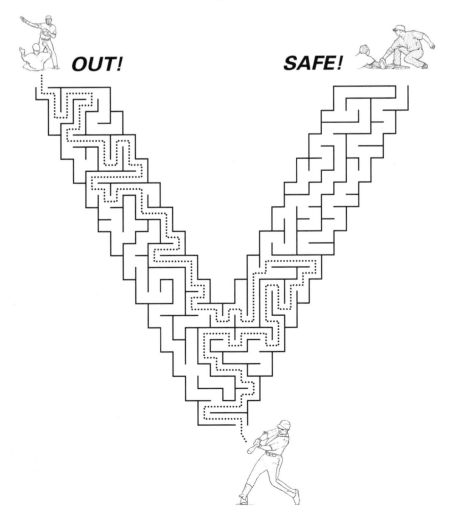

OUT!   SAFE!

Page 45

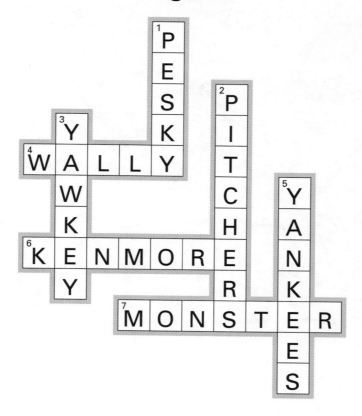

Page 47